Careers in Fashion

Bonnie Szumski

San Diego, CA

ReferencePoint
Press®

LIBRARY OF CONGRESS CATALOGING-IN-PUBLICATION DATA

Szumski, Bonnie, 1958–
    Careers in fashion / by Bonnie Szumski.
        pages cm.—(Exploring careers series)
    Includes bibliographical references and index.
    Audience: 9 to 12.
    ISBN-13: 978-1-60152-704-2 (hardback)
    ISBN-10: 1-60152-704-7 (hardback)
    1. Fashion—Vocational guidance—Juvenile literature. I. Title.
TT507.S995 2015
746.9'2023—dc23
                                                                    2014006483

Contents

The Big Break?

While the most celebrated fashion careers are in fashion and costume design, the fashion industry includes many other careers. For example, textile designers design the patterns on fabric, milliners design hats, and other designers work with jewelry and handbags. Other careers include assistants who help designers, fashion photographers, and fashion magazine editors; assistants shop for supplies and help these professionals in various other ways. It takes many people to successfully manage a fashion show or a photo shoot, for example. In addition, fashion is a retail business, and there are many careers that are involved in making it successful. Buyers, merchandisers, retailers, and sales assistants all contribute to the sale of fashions.

Many careers in fashion seem to be very similar to other careers that rely on raw artistic talent and being in the right place at the right time. Successful people in fashion tell similar stories to those told by well-known actors, painters, and musicians. While all might be talented and work hard, most describe a moment when they were able to get that first big break that allowed them to enter this extremely competitive industry. Fashion designer Rachel Roy, for example, describes on the *Teen Vogue* website the day in 2006 when her big break occurred, bringing her in contact with well-known fashion designers. "André Leon Talley came in unexpectedly during a sales market to view my collection. Upon seeing it, he suggested Anna Wintour see it, too." Roy continues, "The next thing I knew, I was at the Vogue offices presenting my collection on two models." The story seems to be repeated over and over—budding designers, photographers, or bloggers have a brush with fame and the next thing they know, they've hit it big.

Years of Hard Work

These stories can be discouraging for someone who wants to start out in fashion because they seem to suggest that you can only make it if you know someone influential in the industry. But those who investigate further will find that these are not the only stories. For most people, breaking into fashion takes years of hard work, determination, and a lot of rejection. On the *Teen Vogue* website, Steven Kolb, the CEO of Fashion Designers of America, argues that the years of hard work are the reality: "There are no big breaks. It is little cracks along the way that further a person's career. Every little success you have is added to the next success." In other words, wannabe fashionistas who follow their passion, who do not settle for anything less, who put in time and effort will eventually land their dream career.

Many fashion industry insiders are willing to impart advice about how to enter their field. Their stories are as varied as any other artistic profession. Many did not, for example, go to a fashion school; rather, they opted for a liberal arts degree. Fashion designer Whitney Port describes her fashion journey on *Teen Vogue*'s website this way:

> I knew I wanted to attend USC, but they didn't offer a fashion major. I decided to focus on gender studies so I could learn more about the history of how men and women have worked together and separately to create equality. As a female designer and businesswoman, the studies helped me realize how important women's empowerment is. I feel that the balance between what I learned through my jobs and internships in the fashion world paired with the studies and knowledge I gained from USC was a great base to help me in my career and my designs.

Some College Is Recommended

While some fashion professionals, such as designers Ralph Lauren and Steve Madden, did not attend any college, most fashion professionals recommend at least some college. Port, for instance, later went to art college and pursued sculpture and other visual arts. Because technical skills and knowledge form the basis of many fashion industry jobs, most in the industry emphasize the importance of learning

Fashion Industry Facts

The US fashion industry grew 4 percent in 2011, yielding total sales of $199 billion.

More than 4 million people are employed by the US fashion industry.

Although employment in the US apparel manufacturing industry declined by more than 80 percent (from 900,000 to 150,000 jobs), labor productively more than doubled from 1987 to 2010.

New York and California have the highest concentration of fashion designers.

Men's, women's, and children's apparel sales increased by 4 percent, 3 percent, and 6 percent respectively in 2011.

In 2011 manufacturer-owned stores experienced the highest growth rate of 15 percent, followed by specialty stores which increased by 6 percent; department stores grew by 3 percent.

In 2010 each American household spent on average $1,700 on apparel and footwear.

6.9 million women in the United States shop for apparel online.

Approximately 58 percent of women who shop for apparel online are between the ages of 25 and 45.

The United States is the largest importer of garments in the world.

China manufactures 35 percent of all apparel sold in the United States.

Fashion week in New York City funnels approximately $20 million into the country's economy.

Sources: BusinessVibes, "Twelve Facts on the Fashion Industry in the United States," October 2, 2012. www.businessvibes.com; NPD Group, "NPD Reports on the U.S. Apparel Market 2011," March 29, 2012. www.npd.com.

those essential skills and developing a knowledge base. Photographers, for instance, need to have strong knowledge of digital cameras and software techniques. Designers need to understand sewing, construction, and fabric. Style writer Andrew Bevan chose a traditional route—journalism—to enter his writing career, as he described in another story on the *Teen Vogue* website:

> I think my college education prepared me a lot for my career in fashion journalism. I got great basic writing skills from my teachers who were working journalists, and studying both narrative and documentary films really helped me become a more visual person. My internships at Ralph Lauren and Charlie Rose's talk show really gave me hands-on experience. And last but not least, I worked a lot of retail when I was in college and I always say to anyone interested in getting into the fashion industry: never underestimate the power of working in retail. It's the best way to understand how people shop and what clothes they are drawn to, and it's great training to become a people person.

People in the industry frequently talk about passion—passion for fashion, fabric, clothing, images—a passion that grows with them from a very early age. These artistic people find something deeply satisfying in their work with fashion and a connection with the people they meet in the fashion world. Many in the industry say that they simply could not—and would not—do anything else. Passionate about fashion? The careers highlighted in this book capture just a few of the many ways you can turn that enthusiasm into a satisfying career.

Fashion Designer

What Does a Fashion Designer Do?

A fashion designer's duties vary greatly depending on the type of industry, the type of job, and the type of products on which he or she decides to focus. For example, the fashion industry identifies some main areas of clothing design: menswear, women's wear, haute couture, ready-to-wear, and designer fashions, but there are others. Just a few recognized areas include knitwear, sportswear, children's clothing, evening wear, and lingerie. And that's just clothing. Designers also can work in jewelry, handbags, shoes, and hats. Also considered to be within the designer trade are fashion forecasters, who focus on picking trends for design houses. Other fashion designers produce their own labels, either as full-time employees or as independent contractors working for a particular design house. A contract fashion designer can, for example, design one item—such as a dress—for one label and other items for other labels.

No matter where or what they work on, however, the work of fashion designers follows a typical chronology. A fashion designer must study the trends in fashion and understand what would appeal to a customer. He

At a Glance:

Fashion Designer

Minimum Educational Requirements
Bachelor's degree in fashion design or fashion merchandising recommended

Personal Qualities
Artistic; good communication skills

Certification and Licensing
None

Working Conditions
Mostly indoors; some travel may be required

Salary Range
$57,950 to $78,590, with a median of $62,860

Number of Jobs
22,300

Future Job Outlook
Projected 3 percent decline through 2022

or she may cultivate a particular customer or group of customers and design for their needs. On the website Jobstr.com, the fashion designer for NYC Fashionista talks about the clothing line she has created and to whom she sees it appealing: "I design a line of knitted accessories with a contemporary, 'design-forward' aesthetic—think your funky high school art teacher who suddenly has a corporate job and needs something sophisticated she can wear everyday while still expressing her flair and individuality." Handbag designer Rebecca Minkoff agrees that listening to and cultivating customers is an important part of what a fashion designer does. Establishing communication with customers and making them feel a part of the decision-making process has been important to Minkoff's success. She regularly tweets with her twenty-three thousand followers on Twitter and exchanges comments with her sixteen thousand fans on Facebook. She also maintains a website called Minkette, an online forum for her customers. In an interview on the website Entrepreneur, she says, "If someone writes in and tells us the strap on a particular bag isn't long enough to wear in the winter when she's wearing a coat, we'll make the bag with a longer strap the next season. . . . My customers know I'm listening and responding."

Along with studying trends, a fashion designer must also decide on a theme for his or her collection. Inspiration can come from anywhere, and it is usually the key to getting recognition from the fashion community. Child actors turned fashion designers Mary-Kate and Ashley Olsen, for example, quoted in the Associated Press: The Big Story website, say the inspiration for one of their collections came from "the 18th century scrolls of Ito Jakuchu, depicting the Japanese traditions of bird-and-flower paintings."

Once a designer has an inspiration, he or she must develop that inspiration by designing and making some sample products. While many designers continue to design by hand, many others now use computer-aided design (CAD) programs. These programs allow designers to sketch with virtual models and switch colors, shapes, and patterns. After they have an initial idea, fashion designers try out various fabrics and produce a prototype, often with less expensive material than will be used in the final product. They work with models to see how the design will look and adjust the designs as needed. These samples are then photographed and sent to editors or are tested out in trade and fashion shows. Depending on the response that they get in these initial steps, designers may revamp a design or discard it. Sometimes a particular star picks up a designer's early efforts. Having a star such as Lady Gaga wear a piece of a designer's clothing or shoes can make the designer an overnight success. Avant-garde designer Noritaka Tatehana, in an interview on LanciaTrendVisions.com, talks of his relationship with Lady Gaga: "I have a client who is . . . a performer who knows more about my shoes than I do. She has ordered 25 pairs so far. Who do you think it is? Yes, it's Lady Gaga. She is one of my partners in crime and I've grown a lot thanks to her. I think it's not my shoes but my clients that allow me to grow and develop."

How Do You Become a Fashion Designer?

Education

Unlike many careers, a college education is not required in fashion, though it is highly recommended. Most designers recommend two schools in New York City: Parsons and the State University of New York's Fashion Institute of Technology (FIT), although other schools offer fashion design programs throughout the United States. One of these is the Fashion Institute of Design and Merchandising (FIDM) in Los Angeles, California. Various degrees are offered.

Another common strategy is to attend a four-year liberal arts college and then go on to fashion school. Most students take classes in math, business, design, sketching, art history, costume history, literature, pattern making, clothing construction, and textiles. On Examiner.com, fashion designer Gloria Edwards recommends paying for supplemental classes: "I paid for weekly sewing and pattern making classes before attending FIDM to get my degree in fashion design."

Volunteer Work and Internships

The fashion world relies on interns and volunteers, and it is a virtual requirement to volunteer in order to meet people and obtain a job. A posting on the job website Indeed indicates the requirements for such an intern: "Fashion Intern Needed: Assisting our production manager with the production of the Spring/Summer 2014 collection. Assisting Morgan and the assistant designer with the development of the Autumn/Winter 2014 collection. Contributing to social media outlets to reinforce brand recognition and assist in sales. We are a small studio composed of a few people working and designing closely together." Educators recommend asking teachers about possible internships as well as going online to find such opportunities.

Skills and Personality

Most designers agree that creativity and a passion for fashion are not the only requirements for becoming a designer. It is essential to be persistent, even pushy. Designers often meet with a lot of rejection,

A fashion designer fits one of his designs (inspired by a traditional Chinese-style dress) on a model. Designers study fashion trends and contemplate possible themes and influences that will give their work a unique and appealing character.

so a person in the profession has to have a thick skin and be willing to try and try again. On Examiner.com, designer Edwards maintains,

> Be strong, people can be really mean in this industry, especially if you are really talented. Believe and watch out for haters. I have dealt with a lot of meanness in this industry. . . . Try not to let it get to you and surround yourself with people who are like you. If your dreams are big, you need to be around good people who want to see you succeed which has been difficult for me in this industry. My talent and designs speaks for itself. Surround yourself with people who think on your level and who are good energy. . . . Weed the bad ones out.

In addition, most fashion designers consider themselves to be extroverts—and many believe it is a requirement if one is to fight his or her way into such a competitive industry.

On the Job

Employers

According to the Bureau of Labor Statistics (BLS), most fashion designers work in wholesale or manufacturing establishments, apparel companies, retailers, theater or dance companies, and design firms. About 25 percent of fashion designers were self-employed in 2012. These designers often custom-make apparel for clients. In 2012, according to the BLS, the following industries employed the most designers: Apparel (clothing), piece goods (fabrics), and notions (buttons, zippers, ribbon, etc.) merchant wholesalers employed 28 percent of designers and apparel manufacturers employed 17 percent. In addition, 12 percent were employed as managers of companies, 5 percent worked for specialized design services, and 2 percent worked in wholesale electronic markets (business-to-business e-commerce) as agents and brokers. Most designers must travel as part of their job; sometimes this travel takes them to trade and fashion shows or to countries that supply materials and manufacturing workers. The fashion industry is centered at either end of the country, so most work in New York City, Los Angeles, or San Francisco, though some designers work in Chicago.

Working Conditions

Fashion designers usually work full time, and the job is indoors and can involve long hours—especially before a collection is ready to present or before a fashion show. The industry is highly competitive and stressful.

Bra designer Victoria chronicled her typical day in *The Fashion Careers Guidebook*. Victoria has designed for Victoria's Secret. She spends her morning on concept development, selecting fabrics, colors, prints, and trim and making a concept board with photos and swatches, then sketching her designs. She then meets with a design studio that builds her bras so that she can have samples made by the afternoon. In the afternoon she meets with models to present and wear her samples, and then her samples are revised. Finally, by the end of the day, she prepares a spec package for the factory in China where her designs will be produced.

Earnings

According to the BLS, in May 2012 the median annual wages for fashion designers in the top five industries were as follows: management of companies and enterprises, $78,590; specialized design services, $62,560; apparel manufacturing, $62,390; apparel, piece goods, and notions merchant wholesalers, $60,590; and wholesale electronic markets and agents and brokers, $57,950.

Opportunities for Advancement

Beginning designers often work as assistant designers or cutting assistants. From there, they may advance to the positions of pattern designer, technical designer, and, finally, lead designer. *The Fashion Careers Guidebook* offers the example of Sue, who works with a designer for a large footwear company. Sue's first big break after college was customizing shoes. A fashion designer liked her shoes so much that he asked her to design the shoes to go with his fashions for a show, where they would be modeled on the runway, or catwalk. This allowed her to get experience and make some contacts. She now works on two collections that are offered by large department stores throughout the United States.

What Is the Future Outlook for Fashion Designers?

The market for fashion designers will always remain small, and pressure from international manufacturers and designers is expected to grow. As a result, employment of fashion designers in the apparel manufacturing industry is projected to decline 51 percent from 2010 to 2020.

However, designers will still be needed to design clothing and accessories for the mass market and ready-to-wear. Clothing technology, too, improves the outlook for fashion designers, who will be needed to create garments and accessories using the new fabrics.

The fashion industry is very serendipitous, however, and so opportunities will always exist for those with an education in fashion design, excellent portfolios, and industry experience. The direct-to-market online world may also increase opportunities for designers, especially for those who design accessories or one-of-a-kind clothing. For most aspiring fashion designers, moving to California or New York is a necessity since the vast majority of jobs can be found there.

Find Out More

Costume Designers Guild (CDG) Local #892
11969 Ventura Blvd., 1st Floor
Studio City, CA 91604
phone: (818) 752-2400
fax: (818) 752-2402
e-mail: cdgia@cdgia.com
website: http://costumedesignersguild.com

The CDG Local 892 of the International Alliance of Theatrical and Stage Employees represents costume designers, assistant costume designers, and costume illustrators working at the highest levels of skill and expertise in motion pictures, television, and commercials. The CDG promotes and protects the economic status of its members while improving working conditions and raising the standards for its craft.

Council of Fashion Designers of America, Inc. (CFDA)
65 Bleecker St., 11th Floor

New York, NY 10012
website: http://cfda.com

The CFDA is a not-for-profit trade association whose membership consists of more than four hundred of America's foremost women's wear, menswear, jewelry, and accessory designers.

Custom Tailors and Designers Association of America (CTDA)
42732 Ridgeway Drive
Broadlands, VA 20148
phone: (888) 248-2832
e-mail: info@ctda.com
website: www.ctda.com

The CTDA is the oldest continuously operated trade organization in the United States. It is a member association of distinguished master tailors, designers, custom clothiers, and luxury retailers who create custom clothing for clients throughout the United States.

Fashion Group International, Inc. (FGI)
8 W. Fortieth St., 7th Floor
New York, NY 10018
phone: (212) 302-5511
website: www.fgi.org

The FGI is a nonprofit professional organization whose mission is to be the preeminent authority on the business of fashion and design and to help its members become more effective in their careers. To do this, the FGI provides insights on major trends in person, online, and in print; access to business professionals; and a gateway to the influence fashion plays in the marketplace.

National Association of Schools of Art and Design (NASAD)
11250 Roger Bacon Dr., Suite 21
Reston, VA 20190
phone: (703) 437-0700
website: http://nasad.arts-accredit.org

NASAD is an association of 323 schools of art and design, primarily at the collegiate level, but also including postsecondary nondegree-granting schools for the visual arts disciplines. The association produces statistical research, provides professional development for leaders of art and design schools, and engages in policy analysis.

Textile Designer

The textile design profession encompasses many parts of the textile industry but consists of two primary categories: apparel, which encompasses clothing; and interior design, which includes sheets, linens, furniture, and other household products. Textile designers are involved in the design of yarns and fabrics that are used in both apparel and interior design. These individuals create the textile concept or product design, and they also may focus on designing the furnishings and tapestries for a room.

A textile designer needs to develop fabric for any piece of textile machinery. This means they have to select the fiber type, yarn size, and construction method to match the intended use of the fabric. Scott Manley, a technical designer for a textile and chemical company, says on the College Foundation of North Carolina website that designing velour fabric for automotive seating, for example, involves a variety of tasks: "I am involved heavily in sample scheduling, production troubleshooting, cost reduction, machinery evaluations, new process evaluations and competitor research."

At a Glance:

Textile Designer

Minimum Educational Requirements
Associate's or bachelor's degree

Personal Qualities
Artistic; understand color combinations; study fashion trends

Certification and Licensing
None

Working Conditions
Mostly indoors

Salary Range
$32,420 to $79,758

Number of Jobs
Approximately 22,000, hard data unavailable

Future Job Outlook
Jobs will increase by 1 percent through 2018

Once a designer does the legwork on cost, machinery selection, and other particulars, he or she pitches the design to a manager or client. If it is approved, the textile designer often must work with the weaving mill and the client to ensure that the product meets the client's expectations. The designer may have to work with the mill's limitations on color or pattern weave, for example, and offer solutions and compromises. Designers who work in large companies or design houses may specialize in a particular area, such as textile colorist. A colorist chooses color combinations for different fabrics. Another specialty within the field is the CAD artist, who digitizes the fabric design and readies it for the mill.

Rachel Doriss, a textile designer for the Pollack design studio in New York City, describes her typical day on the *L Magazine* website:

> I work very closely with the other designers in the studio. We discuss (in detail) patterns, colors, yarn choices, weave structures for all of the fabric projects in work. Some days I will be drawing a repeat or specifying yarn colors (which can take one full day), and some days I am emailing our weaving mills detailed instructions for how to weave a fabric and which yarns to use. We often meet with our European suppliers who travel to New York to show us the latest yarns and constructions they are weaving with. Textile design can become highly detailed and we pride ourselves on our attention to detail in all of our fabrics.

How Do You Become a Textile Designer?

Education

Textile designers often pursue either an associate's degree or a bachelor's degree, such as a bachelor of fine arts, a bachelor of arts in design, or a bachelor of arts in textile design. In a typical textile design program, students learn about different yarns, fibers, fabrics, and dyes. They also learn about the color and texture of fabric and the history of textiles, and they create sketches and prints. Likewise, textile design students spend time in studios learning how to use digital media,

Designers work with fabric samples at a textile factory. Textile designers are involved in the design of yarns and fabrics, making selections based on patterns, colors, weave structures, and more.

including CAD programs, to design. They also must take courses in weaving and printing equipment as well as courses in merchandising and marketing.

Volunteer Work and Internships

Because of the highly competitive nature of all fashion-related jobs, internships and volunteer opportunities are considered essential for a career in textile design. Many large design houses hire students for both paid and unpaid internships. Companies such as Abercrombie & Fitch, J.C. Penney, Urban Outfitters, and Target actively recruit graduating students from the best design schools for their training programs, which can be unpaid or pay a small salary. Programs usually last three to six months, and during this time companies will evaluate students as possible hires. Design schools often pride themselves on the number of internships and volunteer positions they can find for their current students, and any student in a degree program in fashion should frequent the career planning and placement office.

On the website for North Carolina State University's College of Textiles, for example, the college boasts of its students' internships, including many who interned at large design houses. Meghan Blohm, a fashion and textile student, worked at Isaac Mizrahi in New York City:

> In this internship . . . I learned a lot about different fabrics, how to purchase them from a large textile mill, and which goes best for which designs. I also learned how to trace out patterns and present production layouts. On the sales side of things, I met with buyers and personal shoppers for large stores such as Bergdorf Goodmans for fittings, personal styling, and sales. . . . I was able to help create look books, style boards, flats with fabric swatches. I was preparing the spring line for this upcoming season alongside the employees.

Other internships mentioned on the site included going to Africa to help students make their own clothing and set up a cottage industry.

Skills and Personality

A textile designer must be an artist with a creative side. In addition, he or she must have a love of fashion, a good eye for color, and an understanding of garments and their construction, or, if on the home goods side, a good eye for furniture, window treatments, and other items that might be used together in a home. Other skills required of a textile designer include technical skills, such as knowledge of artist tools, industrial machinery, and various artistic media such as drawing, painting, and printing. Creative skills include the ability to find and identify inspiration and a desire to pursue a creative career. On the Freunde von Freunden website, textile designer Isabel Wilson discusses the need to build a "visual library" for inspiration: "I think it's essential to take in your surroundings, to collect and build a unique visual library. I collect things to allow myself to express the truth about my unconscious mind. I find that my collections inform my work and remind me of what I'm attracted to."

A textile designer must be flexible—able to work alone or with groups of designers to create a product. Because the industry is competitive and includes many people with strong ideas and opinions, textile designers must be good self-marketers and not fear offering their ideas for others to consider. In addition, textile designers must be able to accept rejection without feeling crushed and to keep an optimistic attitude.

Knowing how to use social media to introduce one's designs to the outside world is a big advantage, especially for freelancers and small design companies. Textile and interior designer Caitlin Wilson, who runs her own textile business, says on the Everygirl website,

> I absolutely consider social media to be the reason for the success we've had. The internet is such an incredible tool for creative professionals. In the past, designers could only be seen through print magazines and word of mouth. Social media has changed our field drastically—allowing us to share ideas and make connections with other creatives and businesses to help each other succeed and be seen. . . . I would not have had the ability to market myself as easily (or really at all) without my blog, Pinterest, Instagram, and Facebook.

Textile designers must also have a good idea of the style trends and understand what, and for whom, they are designing. Textile designers need to discuss, understand, and interpret the needs, ideas, and requirements of their customers. They must consider how the textile will be used so that they can understand what properties it must have before producing sketches and samples to present to their customers. For example, when designing bedding, the fabric must be durable and washable, with a print that can withstand wear and tear. Yet the sheets should be soft and pliable, warm for the winter, or cool to the touch for summer.

On the Job

Employers

Textile designers work in textile mills, apparel manufacturers, retail companies, greeting card companies, and tile and dinnerware manufacturers. They can also work with companies that design sheets, pillows, draperies, carpets, and furniture. These companies seek designers to develop and create the style and design of their products and also to work with those involved in the manufacturing process of the products. Two job ads taken from the website Indeed show the types of jobs that may be available for textile designers. For example, Bealls Department Store in Bradenton, Florida, is looking for someone to work "with the design team and contribute design and designs based on Florida consumers' unique merchandise needs. Textile print design experience preferred." Another ad for the kitchen and cookware retailer Williams-Sonoma asks for a designer for kitchen soft goods and textiles. The company wants someone who can "translate trends into concepts that respond to business needs (e.g., price points and geographic considerations)."

Working Conditions

Textile designers usually work normal office hours, though some overtime may be required to meet deadlines. Freelance and self-employed designers may work from home and set their own hours. Designers are usually based in a well-lit office or studio and may spend many hours a day in front of a computer. They may also spend time on a factory floor, checking designs in production. They sometimes attend customer and trade shows. Many textile designers travel overseas to Asia to meet with manufacturers of textiles.

Earnings

According to salary estimator Glassdoor, the average salary for a textile designer in the United States is $50,000. Hard statistics on salaries are difficult to obtain for textile designers because they work in so many different industries and hold many different jobs.

Opportunities for Advancement

Textile designers often move from designing a product to managing production of the product in mills and/or overseas. They may become lead designers on projects that are coordinating a line of products. Many textile designers break out on their own to design their own products and lines or work freelance for large design houses.

What Is the Future Outlook for Textile Designers?

The area of textile design is very competitive, and there will always be more designers than jobs in the United States. Textile designer jobs are found in large fashion-oriented cities, such as New York, Los Angeles, and San Francisco, though freelance opportunities may allow a designer to work from home. Though overseas competition has gutted the textile manufacturing industry in the United States, the future of textile design, though small, remains stable. The BLS predicts that textile designers working in the fashion industry will see an increased demand of only 1 percent through 2018. Design firms that create clothing for mass-market consumption should have the best employment opportunities, while high-end luxury design jobs are much scarcer. However, opportunities to market goods directly to consumers through social media and other outlets remain an unpredictable, and sometimes lucrative, pathway for textile designers.

Find Out More

American Association of Textile Chemists and Colorists (AATCC)
PO Box 12215
Research Triangle Park, NC 27709-2215
phone: (919) 549-8141
website: www.aatcc.org

The AATCC is the world's leading not-for-profit association serving textile professionals. The association provides test-method development, quality-control materials, and professional networking for thousands of members in sixty countries throughout the world.

International Textile and Apparel Association (ITAA)
PO Box 70687
Knoxville, TN 37938-0687
phone: (865) 992-1535
e-mail: info@itaaonline.org
website: http://itaaonline.org

The ITAA is a professional and educational association composed of scholars, educators, and students in the textile, apparel, and merchandising disciplines in higher education. The association welcomes professionals employed in those fields who wish to pursue knowledge, the interchange of ideas, and the dissemination of information through meetings, special events, and publications.

National Council of Textile Organizations (NCTO)
1001 Connecticut Ave. NW, Suite 315
Washington, DC 20036
phone: (202) 822-8028
website: www.ncto.org

The NCTO is a unique association representing the entire spectrum of the textile industry. From fibers to finished products, machinery manufacturers to power suppliers, the NCTO is the voice of the US textile industry. Four separate councils make up the NCTO's four different areas: fiber, yarn, fabric and home furnishings, and industry support.

Surface Design Association (SDA)
PO Box 20430
Albuquerque, NM 87154
phone: (707) 829-3110
website: www.surfacedesign.org

The Surface Design Association is an international community engaged in the creative exploration of fiber and fabric. Its mission is to promote awareness and appreciation of the textile arts. Through member-supported publications, exhibitions, and conferences, the SDA inspires creativity, encourages innovation, and advocates excellence.

Textile Society of America, Inc. (TSA)
PO Box 5617
Berkeley, CA 94705
phone: (510) 363-4541
e-mail: tsa@textilesociety.org
website: http://textilesociety.org

The TSA provides an international forum for the exchange and dissemination of information about textiles worldwide, from artistic, cultural, economic, historic, political, social, and technical perspectives.

Costume Designer

What Does a Costume Designer Do?

Costume designers can work in many artistic media, including film and video, commercials, or in theater. For the most part, they are hired as independent contractors or freelancers, and they usually require an agent to get them hired on jobs.

Costume designers always work as part of a team. Production designers, makeup artists, writers, actors, tailors, costumers, and a director are just some of the people who will be involved in designing the costumes for a production. Costume designers begin their work while the production is in the conceptual stage. They may create new costumes or research and find ready-made wear that will work for the production. Costume designers normally start by reading a script. If a production will take place in a particular historical era, then the costume designer will begin by researching the period. Sometimes that research is difficult. For the 2013 movie *12 Years a Slave*, for example, Academy Award–winning costume designer Patricia Norris explained in an interview on the *Vanity Fair* magazine website how she struggled to figure out how slaves were clothed. Her research led her to understand that slaves wore their masters' castoffs: "Slaves were originally brought over here naked because [merchants] originally wanted to destroy everything that connected them to a past. . . . So you had to figure out where they got their clothes once they got here, like they were castaways."

The costume designer will also meet with the actors to get ideas on what they envision for their character. The designer will then start to make sketches of some of the costumes and bring them to a meeting with the director and design team to get their feedback and ideas. The costume designer will also want to check with the director about how many characters will need costumes, including nonspeaking characters who will be in the background and will also need to be costumed.

Costume designers break down scripts scene by scene in order to work out how many characters are involved and what costumes are required. They then begin the more complex task of developing costume plots for each character. These plots ensure that colors and styles do not mimic each other in the same scene. They also highlight the characters' emotional journeys by varying the intensity and depth of colors and also reflect the mood, tastes, and individuality of each character. Jill Ohanneson, a costume designer for the HBO series *Six Feet Under*, describes how costume design reflects character on the Costume Designers Guild website: "In costume design you're designing for a character. You don't have to just design pants and a shirt and a tie. You're also designing sadness and droopiness and wiltiness. There are so many emotional ways that we play with—color and texture and patterns and the way things hang that contribute to what the character is really about."

A designer's job varies whether he or she is working for a live production, television, or film. For live theater, the costume plot also notes potential problems with costume changes. The designer, director, and wardrobe assistants all need this sort of information well ahead of time because such changes require further planning to make sure the action of the production is not interrupted. While time is not as great a factor in non-live productions, costume changes still mean allowing characters to leave filming to attend to their outfits.

Upon approval of the initial sketches, the costume designer works on the final design boards, producing the sketches in full color. These sketches may be accompanied by fabric swatches or samples, and they will show whatever accessories the costume designer thinks are needed. Accessories may include canes, hats, gloves, shoes, jewelry, or masks. These costume props add to a character's unique personality.

The job of costume designers is not all creativity, however. They must adhere to strict budgets and deadlines. They must keep accurate financial records, usually in the form of weekly expenditure reports. They must also project accurate production schedules. They are in charge of hiring and deciding on salaries for suppliers, costume makers, and assistants. They also arrange costume fittings for actors and extras. If the budget allows and the work is sufficiently difficult, designers can decide to have a dedicated costume workshop where all costume design happens in one area. At the end of a production, costume designers are responsible for archiving the costumes as well as returning costumes that they borrowed or rented for the production.

Once a production airs, the costume designer's role fades into the background. The overall responsibility for day-to-day production is taken over by the wardrobe assistant, who is responsible for maintaining the costume designer's vision and ideas for the production.

The costume designer's day is hectic and endlessly varied. As television costume designer Cameron Daly observes on the *Hollywood Reporter* website, "Every day is so different and unique it's impossible to ever be bored. Reading a new script every week and considering the challenges and how to overcome them and create something beautiful is exciting. My day can include such a broad spectrum of activities, from a trip to Barneys [luxury department store], fitting gladiators, to sketching out molecular cell costumes for a musical."

How Do You Become a Costume Designer?

Education

Costume designers need no formal education, but since the field is highly competitive, many begin with a bachelor's degree in fashion

A plumassier, *a designer who specializes in plumed or feathered costumes and accessories, crafts costume parts in her workshop. Costume designers create new costumes or research and find ready-made wear that will work for a production.*

design, costume design, textiles, or a related degree. These degrees will expose students to the history of costumes, clothing construction, and analyzing characters. Some schools offer certificate programs, usually two-year courses of study that focus on costume design. Even in high school, students can begin to build experience by creating and designing costumes for school plays. Costume designer Cameron Daly describes her educational experiences at University of California, Berkeley (sometimes called "Cal") and beyond: "At Cal I studied art and costume design as well as gender studies. I always knew I wanted to move to New York and study at Parsons and pursue costume and clothing design. While at Parsons, I interned on [the film] *The Nanny Diaries*."

Volunteer Work and Internships

As with other highly competitive fashion jobs, work experience of any kind, whether volunteer or an internship, will give a new costume designer a way of showing initiative and aid in presenting a portfolio.

Some budding costume designers work as assistants to costume designers or personal shoppers—doing some of the legwork for them. One student who got an internship through the website Global Experiences is working as an assistant for a costume designer in Italy: "We were working on the opera called 'Tosca' and a few other little ballets; now we are working on Anna Bolena, which I must say the costumes are soooooo gorgeous. So we prepare costumes for them all. Some are sent in from other cities and we just have to adjust them to the singer, other costumes we have to make."

Skills and Personality

Costume designers must be willing to work hard, for long hours, often for little pay. They must be resourceful, creative, and good at working on a team. Costume designers must also be willing to work within budgets and meet strict deadlines. They must be good with people from varied backgrounds and comfortable working in a leadership role. They must motivate a crew to get things done and negotiate with vendors to meet budgetary constraints. They must also enjoy working independently as a freelancer or contractor, without a regular salary or benefits.

On the Job

Employers

Costume designers are employed by theaters, film producers, ad agencies, and dance companies. A sample of a few employers on the website Indeed lists jobs for the American Film Institute, Walt Disney Parks and Resorts, as well as smaller theater and film companies, including Stone Street Studios and Kai Zhang films. One such ad on EntertainmentCareers.Net asks for a person to work in costume design and wardrobe for Irish Whiskey Productions in Los Angeles: "Full Time Job Seeking Costume Designer/Wardrobe Supervisor for an independently funded art/dance feature film that will require possible original designs." Many traditional routes into costume design include becoming a personal assistant to an assistant costume designer, working on commercial advertising, and/or working on very small independent films or theater productions. Some costume designers have described writing to designers they admire from film and theater and asking to meet them, interview them, or seek out their advice.

Working Conditions

Because most costume designers work on a freelance or contract basis, the job has a high amount of unpredictability when first starting out. The work is stressful, often pays poorly, and involves long hours. According to Shmoop.com,

> It can take a while to reach the top of your craft, so be prepared to put in some very lean years working as a stitcher or pattern maker. . . . However, there is a ton of work to be had in Hollywood—even if you can't get a gig as a head costume designer for a little bit, there are many other costumers working in each production's costume department, so if you stick with it and start working for major studios, you can eventually be making 50k or more a year.

Earnings

Because costume designer jobs vary so much and because many are done on a contract basis, pay also varies markedly. Some costume designers earn somewhere around $33,000 a year (or even less), while others, especially those who have established good reputations in the industry, might earn $100,000 a year or more. Some freelance costume designers are paid per garment, and all are paid in three installments—at the start, after completion of a number of garments, and at the end of the job.

Opportunities for Advancement

Since most costume designers start out working for other costume designers or assistant costume designers, the plum job is to become a lead costume designer on a production. Lead costume designers hire their own teams and are responsible for the entire project. So it is possible for someone who is talented and learns all aspects of the trade to eventually become a lead designer. But it takes perseverance and patience.

What Is the Future Outlook for Costume Designers?

Most sources see the need for costume designers as remaining stable or declining. The work is unpredictable and dependent on the funding of artistic companies and productions. Though there is plenty of work for those in the production area of films and theater, there are only a limited number of costume designers, and those jobs are highly coveted and competitive.

Find Out More

Costume Designers Guild (CDG) Local #892
11969 Ventura Blvd., 1st Floor
Studio City, CA 91604
phone: (818) 752-2400
fax: (818) 752-2402
e-mail: cdgia@cdgia.com
website: http://costumedesignersguild.com

The CDG is part of the International Alliance of Theatrical and Stage Employees. The guild represents costume designers, assistant costume designers, and costume illustrators in motion pictures, television, and commercials. The CDG promotes and protects the economic status of its members while improving working conditions and raising standards for the craft.

Costume Society of America (CSA)
390 Amwell Rd., Suite 402
Hillsborough, NJ 08844
phone: (800) 272-9447
e-mail: national.office@costumesocietyamerica.com
website: www.costumesocietyamerica.com

The CSA advances the global understanding of all aspects of dress and appearance. The society works to stimulate scholarship and encourage study in the rich and diverse field of costume. The CSA serves it members and promotes its goals with national symposia and publications, including the annual journal *DRESS*.

National Costumers Association
6000 E. Evans Ave., #3-205
Denver, CO 80222
phone: (800) 622-1321
e-mail: office@costumers.org
website: www.costumers.org

The National Costumers Association is a professional organization promoting the artistic, historical, educational, and social nature of costuming and the maintaining of ethical business standards.

United States Institute of Theatre Technology (USITT)
315 S. Crouse Ave., Suite 200
Syracuse, NY 13210-1844
phone: (800) 938-7488
website: www.usitt.org

The USITT connects performing arts design and technology communities to ensure a vibrant dialogue among practitioners, educators, and students.

Model

At a Glance:

Model

Minimum Educational Requirements
None

Personal Qualities
Female models: long legs, long waist, slim figure; male models: well proportioned, tall, good muscle definition; both: good posture, easygoing nature, patience, perseverance

Certification and Licensing
None

Working Conditions
Varies from indoor studio to outdoor photo shoots in all sorts of weather. Most jobs are freelance, part-time, and unpredictable. Models can experience periods of unemployment.

Salary Range
Median wage is $15,960 to $43,840 a year

Number of Jobs
4800

Future Job Outlook
15 percent growth projected through 2022

A model works for a client, usually freelance, modeling clothing, accessories, and other fashion items. There are several types of modeling, and some are more competitive than others.

Editorial Fashion Model

Other than runway model, this is the category everyone thinks of when they think *model*. Editorial fashion models appear in the pages of fashion magazines such as *Elle*, *Vogue*, *Glamour*, and *Cosmopolitan*. These types of jobs have very strict standards on their models' height and weight. Essentially, all female fashion models in this category must be tall, long-legged, and thin, while male models must be well proportioned, tall, and have good muscle definition. Even after meeting these requirements, fashion models must also fit the look that a particular designer is going for. Many designers have a preference for how a model looks and will hire models that are similar to each other physically.

Runway Model

These models perform live and walk the catwalk or runway at fashion shows. They also have strict physical guidelines. Women must be at least 5 feet 9 inches (175 cm) and men must be 5 feet 11 inches (180 cm), with slim builds that fit standard sizes. They must be able to walk the runway in style and show off a designer's garments to their full effect. Other types of runway models work in smaller, more local fashion shows that typically take place at a mall or particular store. Most runway models emphasize that the job requires lots of hard work. According to model Jodi Kelly, interviewed in the book *Complete Guide for Models*, "Yes, runway work is glamorous, but only for the 30 seconds you're on the runway. Once you step backstage, all the glamour instantly disappears. At lightning speed you're stripped naked, new clothes are put on you, makeup is changed, earrings are pinned into your ears, your hair is re-combed, and then you go out again for another few seconds."

Fashion Catalog Model

Although catalog models also must be slim and photogenic, they may not have to be as tall as the editorial or runway models. Retailers with an online or print catalog hire more models than any other sector in the industry. This is also the steadiest type of work and is well paid. This category of modeling is not as glamorous as the runway or editorial model, as the model is hired for the sole purpose of making the garment present well in a catalog.

A subset of the fashion catalog model is the general catalog. Many of these catalogs cater to people who have a particular lifestyle, such as fitness enthusiasts, or who have a specific body type, such as petite, plus size, or big and tall. These catalogs offer opportunities for models who do not have the conventional shape or looks that are required by other fashion catalogs. These types of models work for a particular type of clothing designer who makes clothing for specialty markets. On the *Elle* magazine website, plus-size model Tara Lynn talked about how, as a teenager, she did not think she could become a model because of her size. She wants other young people to be aware that there is room for larger women:

> I was never skinny, so I always thought that if I was going to model, I'd have to lose a lot of weight. I knew at some point in my late teens that plus-size modeling existed. Based on societal pressures, you think when you're in your teens that by next summer you're going to be able to wear a size 4 or 6, or fit into that bikini you thought would look pretty if you lost 50 pounds. It just didn't occur to me as something that was realistic. You don't want to invest in your size-14 body when you feel bad about it as a teen.

Commercial Model

Commercial models work in a variety of different areas for a variety of different employers. They can pose for print advertisements, catalogs, campaigns, television shows, magazines, trade shows, and other work. This type of model has the widest variety of different looks. Women and men who work in this category do not have to fit the height and weight requirements of many other modeling jobs. This is because the product that is being sold may require different kinds of people. For example, a shampoo ad will require that a model has beautiful hair. An iPod ad will want a model that looks young and hip. A model who portrays a doctor in a hospital ad might be middle aged and look distinguished.

Promotional Model

A promotional model, also known as a promo model, sells a particular brand, product, or service. This category also includes spokesmodels and trade show models. Like the commercial model, a wider range of body type is acceptable, so the field is easier to break into. Since these models may sell the product in print materials, it is important that they look and behave as though they would use the product. Spokesmodels make more money than promo models because they sign exclusive contracts with particular companies and represent those companies at special events, traveling, and in other situations. Trade show models are hired by a company to represent their brand, product, or service at a trade show or convention. They must be outgoing, work well with people, and engage others. They must work long hours and know their company's products well enough to speak knowledgeably about them.

Parts Model

These models have a particular body part—such as hands, legs, or feet—that appeals to advertisers. Hand models are particularly requested. A hand model must have long, graceful hands and fingers with wrinkle-free, clear skin. Nails must also be perfectly shaped and manicured.

A model's hair and makeup are finalized before the start of a fashion show. Whether they work in shows or pose for photo spreads, fashion models must be willing to allow others to make styling decisions.

How Do You Become a Model?

Education

No formal education is required to model. Many in the industry recommend taking some catwalk classes for runway modeling or acting classes to improve acting skills in front of a camera.

Auditions

Most modeling jobs are obtained through auditions at various casting agencies. Models will often have agents that make their clients aware of the ones they think they will best fit, but they are also announced on modeling websites.

Volunteer Work and Internships

As with many other fashion jobs, a modeling internship is considered a necessity to help build a portfolio of pictures and, if possible, photo shoots and to gain exposure to how the career works. Internships are available at talent agencies and modeling agencies; some of these opportunities appear on agency websites. Thatiana Diaz, a Pace University junior at the time she was interviewed by *Seventeen* magazine about her internship at the Wilhelmina modeling agency, said, "My internship has taught me that the modeling world is a really fast changing one. A model that could be 'big' one day can have her fall the next. It is important for models to keep up with the industry they are in and listen to the advice they are given from their agencies so they can continue to make it. I did not realize how much pressure models were under. I have so much respect for them!"

Skills and Personality

Models spend a lot of time waiting, so patience is a must. Models must also tolerate being treated like props. At a photo shoot, others will be styling the model's hair and makeup, with no input from the model. Models must also love city life and traveling, as almost all modeling takes place in large cities. They must also have the perseverance to go from audition to audition without getting the job. While putting up with all of this, a model must be cheerful, polite, and eager to get a shoot the way the photographer and stylist want it. Because models compete with other equally beautiful women and handsome men, they cannot afford to be hard to work with. Photographer Eric Bean comments in *Complete Guide for Models*, "The prima donna 'diva' model is a media myth—with so many beautiful faces to choose from, why would I ever hire someone nasty." In short, passion and a love for fashion and modeling must propel the model.

Some model qualities are more intangible. Models must be photogenic. They must know how to translate direction from a photographer about mood and impression, so they must also be able to act in front of a camera. Many in the industry argue that a model must love the camera. In *Complete Guide for Models*, a fashion model named Carmen talks about this quality: "If you've really got it, it shows in a snapshot. . . . Your mother can get a flattering photo of you with the cheapest camera. You can even put a dollar in one of those photo booths and get a strip of great pictures."

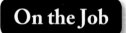

On the Job

Employers

Many models find it a virtual necessity to work through a modeling agency or agent to get work. These agencies and agents are asked by fashion magazines, catalogs, and others for models of certain types, and they refer the models they represent to shoots. In an interview on the Merocrat website, model Samantha Wilkinson describes the most difficult aspects of breaking into the business:

> Finding clients that want to work with you on that first job and then continue to book you. Without an agent I wouldn't find it possible at all, but even with one, the worry is always there, as work comes in waves. One month you could be working so much you don't have a single day off and the next you may not work at all. You've definitely got to be sensible with money and have something ready for the quiet periods so you don't drive yourself mad.

According to the BLS, demand for models is expected to increase as the number of online retailers grows. Employers in the online world who require models include online publications, digital ads, and websites. Businesses may also introduce new advertising campaigns and product launches. These will require models to promote and market products in stores, television commercials, and fashion shows.

Working Conditions

Models' working conditions could challenge endurance athletes. Models must stand for long periods of time while adjustments are made in photo shoots. They wear dozens of outfits and go through frequent hair and makeup changes during a shoot. If they are runway models, the atmosphere is frequently stressful as designers try to make last minute adjustments before the model goes out on the runway.

Earnings

Very few models make the six-figure incomes associated with the supermodels. According to the website College Optional Careers, models in the United States have a median salary of $32,920 a year, or $15.83 an hour. The top 10 percent of models make $43,840 a year or more; the bottom 10 percent make $15,960 a year or less.

Opportunities for Advancement

For models, advancement is not linear as in traditional careers. Advancement is interpreted as working for bigger and better clients and being booked frequently at higher rates. The dream of every model is to become a high-demand supermodel, but that career path is very limited.

What Is the Future Outlook for Models?

According to the BLS, employment of models is projected to grow 15 percent from 2012 to 2022, faster than the average for all occupations. However, because it is a small occupation, the fast growth will result in only about seven hundred new jobs over the ten-year period.

Find Out More

Model Alliance
110 E. Twenty-Fifth St.
New York, NY 10010
e-mail: info@modelalliance.org
website: http:// modelalliance.org

The Model Alliance believes that models deserve fair treatment in their workplace and aims to establish ethical standards that bring real and lasting change to the fashion industry as a whole. The alliance seeks to improve the American modeling industry by empowering the models themselves.

ModelingAdvice
website: www.modelingadvice.com

This website offers lots of interesting information about becoming a model, including information on how to avoid modeling scams.

ModelNetwork, Inc.
website: www.modelnetwork.com

The ModelNetwork provides models with information on how to get started. Its website includes information on how to pick an agency, advice on modeling, and a list of resource material.

ModelNews
website: http://modelnews.com

The site offers a free modeling evaluation, tips on how to become a model, a model-of-the-month contest, a scam watch, and other relevant information.

World Model Association (WMA)
website: www.worldmodel.org

The WMA is the first worldwide cooperative association for model agencies and models. The association connects models to model agencies, photographers, and scouts. The members of WMA benefit from special rates and privileges, which support them in practicing their profession.

Fashion Buyer

What Does a Fashion Buyer Do?

The fashion buyer may work for a small boutique, a department store chain, or a multinational company. Buyers may be responsible for purchasing women's, men's, and children's clothing, mostly wholesale but also retail. They must buy lots of different items, including lingerie, shoes, scarves, belts, jewelry, and other fashion accessories. For a small business, one buyer may make all the decisions. For a larger business, the buyer may work on a team in a corporate office to make the decisions. No matter what size business, a buyer has to know a lot about many parts of the business to do his or her job effectively.

Buyers use style trends and style history to spot the styles that may be coming back into popularity. This involves a bit of seeing into the future because buyers typically make their clothing purchases one to two seasons ahead. To determine upcoming styles, buyers do Internet research and attend fashion designer style shows. Buyers also attend trade shows where different clothing producers show their lines. The buyer decides what are going to be the hot items for the next seasons. If he or she makes an error, the store loses money by stocking styles that no one will buy. As Terry Hughes, a buyer in Georgia, says on the College Foundation of North Carolina website, "Money is always a concern. . . . It's not like a shopping spree because you're ordering out of your business's pocket. If they don't sell, you don't have a business." Spotting trends means having both an artistic flair for clothes and knowledge of the store's customers and what they are most likely to buy. Buying too much or too little can be a problem. Hughes says, "You have to go for the bare minimum if you're not sure about something, but you also don't want to be sold out right away. It takes good decision making."

Buyers must be masters of analyzing inventory, shifting stock between stores, and ordering and reordering items to anticipate what any given store needs. Experience with computer programs that crunch data (such as Excel) is very important to buyers. As Hughes says, "At the most basic level the buyer ensures that the correct merchandise is in a store at the correct time with the correct quantities to satisfy the customer. The success of a buyer is quantified by achievement of retail sales and gross margin goals." Even though fashion buyers rarely work directly with customers, they must also have good people skills. No matter what size the store environment is, buyers work with a lot of people. They must work with wholesalers, retail stores, and other vendors to purchase goods and negotiate prices. They must network to be able to obtain must-have items first. They also must work with their sales team to educate them about new merchandise, encourage and motivate them to sell product, and help with any problems or issues that come up.

Buyers must understand the products they buy for their companies to sell. They must be knowledgeable about the quality of a particular fabric and how a garment will hold up. They must then find a manufacturer that can meet their standards and negotiate the best price to make the most profit for their store. This is a key part in satisfying the customer. In 2013 the yoga clothing manufacturer Lululemon, for example, lost millions of dollars when their buyer made a mistake on a manufacturer and their yoga pants were made with a fabric so sheer that women were returning them in droves.

Most buyers work long hours. It is not uncommon for fashion buyers to work on holidays as well because this is the busiest time of the year for all retailers. Many travel, sometimes overseas, to meet with clothing manufacturers or for fashion shows. The job can be very high pressure, as whether the store is doing well or not largely depends on their analytical skills.

Understanding the world of sales is essential for any good fashion buyer. While fashion buying may seem romantic and artistic, that should not be the reason to begin this career, say many buyers. It is often said that a good sales person should be able to sell anything. The same is true of fashion buyers. The role of the buyer is the same across all businesses, as the skills rely on the same sort of analytical thinking. As a buyer on the Job Shadow website says, "You have to really enjoy business management first and product second and understand that in your career, if you really are truly a good merchant, you should be able to buy widgets, gadgets, and designer clothing exactly the same. You should be as good a buyer buying staple guns for the Home Depot as you are buying Couture."

How Do You Become a Fashion Buyer?

Education

Because the role of buyer involves so much that can be translated into any business, most employers hire buyers who have a degree in business, marketing, or merchandising. Some fashion schools, such as FIT, offer degree programs that are tailored to merchandising and may offer some students a leg up in the career. In general, though, becoming a buyer requires experience. Students interested in this career usually begin by becoming a buyer's assistant to learn the basics of the business. Typically, a buyer's assistant stays in the role from one to three years before becoming a buyer. A fashion buyer interviewed on the website Boutique Buyers followed this path:

> Most fashion buyers start out by working on the shop floor either as sales assistants or shop managers. I was no different and worked on the shop floor for 4 years. This allowed me to get a full understanding of all the designers and merchandise

we stocked, from clothing, bags and accessories to small jewelry items. It also gave me great insight into the many comments we receive, good and bad, direct from customers.

Certification and Licensing

The American Purchasing Society (APS) offers several levels of certification. Though these certificates are not required, some businesses prefer candidates who have them. The APS offers four worldwide certification programs: the Certified Purchasing Professional, the Certified Professional Purchasing Manager, the Certified Green Purchasing Professional, and the Certified Professional Purchasing Consultant.

Volunteer Work and Internships

As in other fashion careers, most employers see internship experience as a must. Department store chains and other fashion outlets offer internships. Websites such as InternMatch list dozens of internships, all of which provide great experience for budding fashion buyers. Some of the programs place interns in positions in retail sales, visual displays, and trend research. Bloomingdale's buyer Eunice Park, quoted on savvysugar.com, followed this route: "I graduated from the University of Michigan with a BA in Economics and was recruited on campus into the Macy's Buying Training Program. I worked in their Minneapolis buying office for about six months. . . . We recruit from schools across the country for our Buying Training Program as well as internships." A buyer interviewed on Job Shadow had a similar beginning:

> My school required a formal internship junior year and the department store [I worked for] agreed to move me to New York to work in their flagship store for a semester as a store-line management intern. After showing strong performance results I was granted a second internship in the buying office the next summer. This buying office internship, in addition to 6 years of part-time retail experience, opened many doors. Upon college graduation, I was given offers in big-box, specialty and department store buying offices.

Skills and Personality

Buyers must be very analytical and understand business. Park says that the ideal buyer candidate is "someone who is outgoing, analytical, and a good multitasker. It also takes someone who can adapt to a fast paced environment." Buyers have very stressful jobs because they are a key part of a business's profitability. Their decisions can make or break a clothing business. And even though the job is stressful, buyers insist that a key part of it is to be friendly, enthusiastic, upbeat, and passionate about the work. Buyers also need to have a high energy level to keep up with their task load.

On the Job

Employers

All major department stores, boutiques, and midsize clothing stores employ buyers. Job postings on the Indeed website include positions with Buffalo Exchange, Free People, and Urban Outfitters.

Working Conditions

Buyers have a lot of variety in their jobs, and their jobs are very stressful. The typical fashion buyer does a little bit of everything. In a small store a buyer might play many roles, including putting up new clothing displays and helping with the lighting and shelving for displays in order to feature merchandise. Buyers may be in the office all day crunching inventory numbers, researching trends by reading fashion and trade magazines, analyzing sales figures, and reading the newspaper headlines trying to anticipate how the economy will affect consumer spending. Or they may be traveling to other stores, meetings, fashion shows, retail trade shows, or going to Asia to research manufacturers. The buyer interviewed on the Job Shadow website argues that the job is far from glamorous: "Maybe 5 out of 200 major style buyers in my company get to do anything remotely like cool, as far as meeting celebrities, going to fashions shows, unique product offering and whatnot. It happens, and it's fun when it does, but it is not as often as people think."

Earnings

Entry-level buyer's assistants typically make anywhere from $35,000 to $42,000 per year. Purchasing managers in department stores earned a mean annual wage of $167,630 in 2011, while those who worked for apparel, piece goods, and notions merchant wholesalers earned $143,870, according to the BLS. Fashion buyers can also receive bonuses based on sales goals. They are typically employed full-time and receive health benefits.

Opportunities for Advancement

Many buyers start out in a buyer training program from a major retailer. Another typical route is to start as a retail sales clerk, learning the retail business. On the Monster website, Connie Passarella, the career services director at FIT in New York City, says sales clerk experience is helpful: "It's not a requirement, but companies like to see retail experience on an individual's resume. . . . That way, they know you have a basic understanding of the selling floor." The next step is to become an assistant buyer, working under the tutelage of the buyer. An assistant usually stays in the position for three to four years. The next career step is associate buyer, a position that typically lasts for approximately two years before one has an opportunity to advance to a buyer position.

What Is the Future Outlook for Fashion Buyers?

The national outlook for buyers is conservative. The BLS says that employment of purchasing managers, buyers, and purchasing agents is projected to grow 4 percent from 2012 to 2022, slower than the average for all occupations. Yet this statistic pertains to all industries, not just fashion. For cities that are fashion centered, the outlook seems more promising. According to the California Occupational Guides, employment for buyers is expected to grow slightly faster than all other occupations taken as a whole. Competition for fashion buyer jobs is stiff, as the job attracts many college graduates. Successful candidates are likely to be well qualified, with internship and retail experience.

Find Out More

American Purchasing Society (APS)
PO Box 256
Aurora, IL 60507
phone: (630) 859-0250
e-mail: propurch@propurch.com
website: www.american-purchasing.com

The APS is a professional association of buyers and purchasing managers and was the first organization to establish certification for buyers and purchasing professionals. The APS offers numerous online purchasing courses, and many of these courses also count as credit toward various certification levels.

Institute for Supply Management (ISM)
2055 E. Centennial Circle
Tempe, AZ 85284
phone: (480) 752-6276
website: www.ism.ws

The ISM is the first supply management institute in the world. The institute leads and serves the supply management profession and is a highly influential and respected association in the global marketplace.

National Association of Retail Buyers & Sellers
PO Box 705
Morristown, NJ 07960
website: www.narbuyers.org

The National Association of Retail Buyers & Sellers is a nonprofit association that aims to unify and organize those retail professionals who desire to further their career and/or education in the retail buying, selling, planning, or product development field. Through formal and informal educational programs, roundtable discussions, and networking events, the association contributes to the professional growth of its members.

National Retail Federation (NRF)
1101 New York Avenue NW #1200
Washington, DC 20005
phone: (202) 783-7971
website: www.nrf.com

The NRF is the world's largest retail trade association, representing discount and department stores, home goods and specialty stores, Main Street merchants, grocers, wholesalers, chain restaurants, and Internet retailers from the United States and more than forty-five countries.

Fashion Writer

Fashion writers can also be called fashion journalists. Fashion writers write for a variety of different print and online sources, including fashion magazines, advertisers, trade publications, newspapers, and online forums and fashion blogs. Some fashion writers join with fashion photographers so that they can add visual images to their stories to increase their chances of selling a piece.

Fashion writers must have great writing and communication skills as well as know a lot about the fashion industry. They must be very good at descriptive writing; after all, they are trying to convey a visual image—fashion—in words. They also must be up on current fashion trends and be able to predict future trends. Fashion writers have many methods to try to stay ahead of trends and report on issues important to the fashion world. Developing strong contacts within the industry is crucial. Contacts help get writers invitations to fashion shows, launch parties, and private viewings by top designers and

At a Glance:
Fashion Writer

Minimum Educational Requirements
None required, though a bachelor's degree in journalism or fashion merchandising is recommended

Personal Qualities
Tenacity; awareness of latest style trends; good networker; outgoing personality

Certification and Licensing
None

Working Conditions
Aggressive deadlines; most writers work as freelancers

Salary Range
$51,500 to $54,500

Number of Jobs
Unknown

Future Job Outlook
Uncertain; very few full-time positions are available; work is mostly on a freelance and commission basis

retailers. A writer who can scoop the competition by offering articles for publication before other writers will likely find more outlets willing to buy his or her stories.

Reporting on the latest fashion trend or writing articles about specific designers or shows are common projects. But some fashion writers take on the hard topics that plague the industry, such as underage models, modeling scams, unrealistic body image portrayed in the fashion industry, and working conditions for models and garment workers. Writers who tackle subjects like these generally have a more investigative focus than those who stick to fashion trends and announcements.

Although their focus is fashion, fashion writers are like other journalists in that they try to convey information, perspective, and emotion in their writing. To do that, they must have an interest in their topics and a desire to learn more about the people and events that influence the industry. Jeanne Beker talks about what she loves about the job on the website Career Bear:

> I think every journalist has to be a storyteller . . . and I love telling stories. . . . I also love the fact that fashion is theatre. My roots were in theatre, I wanted to be an actress, and I find that, as an arena, it just doesn't get more theatrical than the world of fashion, with its grand dramas and its constant crises and larger than life personalities and characters. . . . This job can be glamorous, and it can also be brutally unglamorous. I did not get into it for the glamour. I'm much more intrigued by the grit of it. In fact glamour and travel are not the reasons you should pursue this career. . . . I think it's got to go way, way, way beyond that and for me it's really people. It's totally about people and I love people.

Most fashion journalists would agree that people skills are essential for anyone who wants to do this job. Fashion writers must know the audience for which they are writing. They must know whether the publication is chatty and informal or more traditional, for example. A writer must also pitch ideas and write on topics that will interest a particular publication's readers. A successful fashion writer gets along with and genuinely likes a variety of people. Sometimes knowing the right person may be the difference between selling a piece or not. Finally, networking is very important to fashion writers—as it is with all writers. Those people connections will make a difference and ease the way to getting pieces published.

Many fashion writers believe that it is important to develop a specialty, for example, costumes, and stick with it. Writing about one particular aspect of fashion increases both knowledge base and credibility among readers. In addition, fashion writers need to develop a particular style and point of view to gain followers of their columns and thus gain a reputation. One outlet for fashion writers who want to gain a presence is the fashion blog. The Internet is rife with fashion bloggers who gain readership because their followers want to know what they think, what they are wearing, and what they believe is the next trend. This can lead to advertisers paying bloggers for advertising space on their site, having retailers send them merchandise to review for payment, or landing a book or television deal.

How Do You Become a Fashion Writer?

Education

While no degree is required to become a fashion writer, excellent written and oral communication skills are necessary. One option is to pursue a degree in traditional journalism, which will teach different forms of article writing as well as interviewing techniques. Another route is to obtain an associate's degree in fashion journalism or a bachelor's degree in fashions communication. Schools that offer this degree offer courses in business and marketing, fashion, integrated media, and graphic design.

Volunteer Work and Internships

As with all careers in the fashion industry, internships are a virtual necessity to landing a job, and unpaid work is common. Beth Vincent, the features editor for the menswear website Oki-ni, talked about her internship on MyJobSearch.com. After she graduated with a bachelor's degree in English literature, Vincent applied for the

Vogue Young Talent Competition: "Along with the other finalists, I was invited to attend a lunch at Vogue House where I met some of the writers and editors of the magazine. I was offered a month-long unpaid internship at Vogue, which I took up over the summer." Most internships are not as exciting as Vincent's, however, and may consist mostly of grunt work, including fetching the editors' coffee and filing. One former intern for *West Coast Women's Wear Daily*, however, had a unique view of this mundane job. Kim-Van Deng was quoted in the book *In Fashion*: "It's the most important job in the office. You get to read every piece of paper. . . . I was controlling all the information. . . . I very quickly made myself indispensable."

Skills and Personality

A fashion writer needs excellent written and verbal communication skills. He or she must also have an interest in fashion and the latest trends. Along with these skills, a fashion journalist must know computers. As the future of fashion writing is online, it is essential to learn the software programs and coding that is necessary to post online content. Sarah Cristobal, a senior fashion editor for the website StyleList, writes in the book *In Fashion* that these skills are essential at her job:

> It's a different skill set than what you are taught in J [journalism] school. . . . Learning the technical aspects was akin to learning a different language. . . . Learn about HTML and XML. Familiarize yourself with Facebook, Twitter, Tumblr, and all of those social networking sites which have become so important for media outlets that want to reach a broader audience. Maybe even get your hands dirty and start your own blog.

On the Job

Employers

Most jobs in fashion writing are available in the large fashion cities, including New York City, Los Angeles, London, and Paris. Newspapers such as the *New York Times* have extremely small fashion desks, with only a handful of full-time staff. Glossy fashion magazines such as *Vogue, InStyle,* and *Marie Claire* hire fashion writers, but most writers who work for these magazines work as contractors or freelancers supplying content on an irregular basis. Although print is in decline, opportunity is increasing in the online world. Even the large fashion magazines have an online presence with a need for writers who know how to code their content for online presentation. Many fashion writers work for public relations and advertising agencies developing content as well as writing for newspapers or magazines.

A small number of opportunities are also available in radio and television. These opportunities involve writing for the many reality television shows. Most opportunities in radio and television, however, center on writing advertising copy for fashion products advertised on radio and television.

Working Conditions

Much fashion writing is done the way it has always been done—sitting in front of a computer, trying to come up with creative articles, and meeting aggressive deadlines. When not writing, however, fashion writers are on the go, traveling to important fashion shows, visiting department stores or fashion houses to be briefed on the latest fashions, or attending social functions related to fashion both as a reporter and to network with others.

With the advent of fashion blogs, fashion writers can gain a following that can lead to further writing assignments or even a television show or book. Fashion blogger Leandra Medine recently turned her fashion blog, *The Man Repeller*, into a published book. She describes her typical day as boring:

> I'll get to my computer around 8 or 8:30, set live the first blog post, and then from 9 until 1:30 I'm either working on the second blog post or the next day's blog post or doing market research for whatever it is. . . . I'm essentially doing that until around 2 p.m., and then I set live the second post. It's always two a day. . . . And then it's the same thing from, like, 3 until 6:30 or 7. I'm either working on the next day's post or the following day's post or the editorial calendar.

Earnings

For most fashion writers, developing a career takes time and most starting jobs pay poorly, if at all. According to an article on the *Houston Chronicle*'s website Chron.com, salaries for established fashion writers range from $51,500 to $54,500 a year, though salaries are much lower for beginning writers. Editorial assistants at fashion magazines make much less, in the $20,000 range, but these jobs are considered a springboard to eventual writing jobs. In addition, much fashion writing is done freelance, per piece.

Opportunities for Advancement

A fashion journalist usually begins his or her career by interning (for free or almost nothing) at a print publication. From there, a writer may be able to move up the ranks to contributing writer or editor with the goal of becoming an assistant editor, associate editor, or editor. In television or radio, a writer may move up to become a producer or reporter. Many fashion writers work freelance and sell their stories to a number of publications and outlets. One unconventional but increasingly popular way of gaining a following that may translate into paid work is the fashion blog.

What Is the Future Outlook for Fashion Writers?

The decline of the glossy fashion magazine has led to a lessening of opportunities for beginning fashion writers. Yet at the same time, the industry has experienced an uptick in online fashion publications, including blogs and online magazines, which has in turn created new outlets for writers. The BLS has predicted a decline in the number of writers needed overall, but it does not call out fashion writing specifically.

Association of Magazine Media
810 Seventh Ave., 24th Floor
New York, NY 10019
phone: (212) 872-3700
website: www.magazine.org

The Association of Magazine Media is a nonprofit organization representing magazine media, print and digital. It provides an organized forum in which publishers can advance their common interests. It offers career information and posts internship possibilities.

Fashion Group International, Inc. (FGI)
8 W. Fortieth St., Seventh Floor
New York, NY 10018
phone: (212) 302-5511
website: www.fgi.org

The FGI is a nonprofit professional organization with five thousand members in the fashion industry, including apparel, accessories, beauty, and home. The FGI provides insights on major trends in person, online, and in print; access to business professionals; and a gateway to the influence fashion plays in the marketplace.

Independent Fashion Bloggers
website: http://heartifb.com

This website offers an online community of fashion bloggers and dubs itself the ultimate resource for the fashion blogger to learn about blogging, media kits, fashion, photography, and marketing. It features examples of blogs, a blog of the week, and helpful tips to start a blog.

International Association of Beauty and Fashion Bloggers (iFabbo)
website: www.ifabbo.com

iFabbo is a leading international organization for fashion and beauty bloggers and publishers. To gain membership, each blogger and publisher applicant goes through a vigorous review process. Members must adhere to a strict code of conduct. The association requires bloggers to follow all government regulations and laws.

Fashion Stylist

There are several different types of fashion stylist, and what they do varies greatly. The industry recognizes magazine styling, television styling, music styling, catalog styling, and personal styling as all under the larger rubric of fashion stylist.

At a Glance:
Fashion Stylist

Minimum Educational Requirements
No degree needed; two-year fashion merchandising degree recommended

Personal Qualities
Good organizational skills; interest in fashion and trends; communication and networking skills; resilient; energetic; confident

Certification and Licensing
None

Working Conditions
Lots of travel getting to and from fashion shoots; networking with others in the fashion industry; lots of research on the computer to keep up-to-date on fashion trends

Salary Range
$64,000 to $130,000 per year or $150 to $500 per day

Future Job Outlook
Limited; stylists are hired by the day on a freelance basis

Magazine Stylist

A magazine stylist, also called a fashion editor, usually reports to a creative director or editor in chief of a fashion magazine. Creative directors or editors will normally direct the photo shoots for the cover and articles, telling the stylist what they would like to see in the magazine. Stylists are responsible for procuring the clothes for the shoots. Often they contact designers and retailers to ask about borrowing clothing for the shoot; then they visit in person to make sure the clothing will serve the magazine's purpose. After procuring the clothing, accessories, and shoes for the shoot and gaining approval for the looks, the stylist will participate in the actual shoot. He or she will be in charge of dressing the models and celebrities and will help the makeup and hair stylists with general ideas. After many years working her way up in the magazine business for employers that included *Mademoiselle, Self,* and *Marie Claire,* stylist Amanda Ross became a freelance fashion stylist and eventually ended up in film and television. In the book *In Fashion,* she credits her early years as an assistant with leading to her success: "Working as an assistant under a great editor leads to a wisdom that guides your instincts. You come to trust your good instincts. You become a good problem solver. You begin to understand the bigger picture of a shoot, the story, the magazine, the fashion business."

Television Stylist

A television stylist will work with the producer of a show as well as the stars to buy outfits for the production. He or she will be given a budget and be told to purchase a certain number of outfits. Upon approval of the stylist's choices, she or he will begin the tailoring and accessorizing as required. A television stylist is deeply involved with the show and its characters. If it is a series, then the stylist has an ongoing role in character development.

Music Stylist

Music stylists style musicians for videos and concert tours. Many people might have a say in the performer's style, including the band manager, video producer, and performer. For this reason, the job requires a lot of diplomacy and collaboration. The job also requires resourcefulness. Musicians on tour often live out of their suitcases and rely on hotel laundry services. To prepare for this, music stylists must find ready-to-wear, easy-to-clean, and easy-to-pack garments. Many music stylists consider themselves an important part of making the "brand" that is their band. Nicole Janowicz is a music stylist for the Backstreet Boys. In a guest post on the *Michael Brandvold Marketing* blog she claims that "one of the perks of being a musician is that you have the freedom to play with your wardrobe and use fashion and style to represent both your music and onstage persona. As a stylist, my goal is to use the best the international fashion industry has to offer to create a style and image that is strong, able to evolve with my clients' careers, and most importantly, reflect their individuality."

Catalog Stylist

Catalog stylists work with a catalog director and clothes buyer to assist with photo shoots for clothing catalogs. Though this job is not as creative as many of the others in fashion styling, it does pay well and regularly. In an advertisement on FashionJobsToday.com, one ad describes a job opening for a catalog stylist for HauteLook, a Nordstrom company. The ad states,

> In addition to paid time off and medical, dental, and vision insurance, we offer a fun, casual working environment in Downtown LA. HauteLook is searching for a talented Photo Product Stylist with experience styling off-figure product: handbags, shoes, jewelry and children's merchandise. As a stylist in our studios you will be primarily tasked with preparing and arranging products for online catalog photography. In this position you will: Follow our existing Style Guide. Ensure all merchandise is presented to HauteLook standards. Work well in a collaborative team environment. Integrate their own individual sense of aesthetics as to be able to bring tasteful and efficient ideas to the table. Job Requirements: A superb eye for visual composition and attention to detail. Excellent organizational skills. The ability to prioritize tasks and maintain strict deadlines. Self-driven motivation and ability to communicate and collaborate in a team environment. Productivity focused and proven to be a quick problem solver. Excellent written and oral communication skills. A college degree in Fashion, Visual Merchandising, Design, Photography or related area. Fashion or Product Styling experience, 2 years experience in Retail or as a Visual Merchandiser.

Personal Stylist

The job of a personal or celebrity stylist is possibly one of the most sought-after fashion stylist careers. These stylists work for personal clients, nearly always women, and are in charge of selecting wardrobes for important events, parties, and awards ceremonies. They often play an important part in the amount of attention and type of attention the star receives. These stylists often command large sums of money from their clients to be their personal shoppers and obtain gowns and accessories from top designers. The job requires the ability to network and know the right people to obtain the right gown. These stylists go to fashion shows with their clients in mind, and they are often competing with other stylists to dress their celebrity. The *Hollywood Reporter* claims that the celebrity stylist is so important that he or she "can help cinch a magazine cover, win their client beauty and fashion contracts or even an actress's next role."

How Do You Become a Stylist?

Education

There is no single route to becoming a fashion stylist. Very few schools, even fashion schools, offer a major in the career, though FIT offers a certificate program with 165 hours of coursework that includes required classes in fashion styling for media. Other optional courses include hand sewing, mending and alteration fundamentals, and an introduction to fashion photography. Other companies offer workshops in areas such as vintage clothes shopping or where to obtain fabric, trimmings, and flowers. Other routes to this career include getting a traditional bachelor of arts degree and then interning with a professional stylist.

Volunteer Work and Internships

Because getting started in the stylist business is difficult, most stylists recommend volunteering and interning as much as possible to build a portfolio. Stylist Erica Matthews, in an article featured on the website All About Styling, offers this advice: "Start to build up your portfolio with photographers, make-up artists, hair stylists etc. when you're confident. Research and shadow/assist good stylists. . . . Start to build your relationships with designers and PR agencies etc. It all depends on what type of styling you want to do; print & media (magazines etc.), Music Videos, Personal Styling . . . and just GO FOR IT!!"

Skills and Personality

Like other careers in fashion, the many personality traits of a stylist are rather intangible and more innate than learned. A stylist's sense of style and fashion trends is very subjective and involves skills that cannot be taught. According to *Harper's Bazaar* editor in chief Glenda Bailey, quoted in the book *In Fashion*, "To be a fashion editor [at a magazine, the equivalent of a stylist] you have to have a vision, and you have to be strong enough to fight for your vision. . . . I believe in individual talent. . . . You either have that talent or you don't."

Other skills include organizational skills, grace under pressure, a thick skin, diplomacy, and the ability to get along well with others. Bailey contends that "you have to be able to collaborate with many other strong personalities who are around you to bring your vision to life. Then you have to have hard work and determination. And you have to have enthusiasm, and you have to truly love it because you have to work so hard that if you don't absolutely love it, you don't have a chance." When asked, most stylists also mention that the ability to network is very important to the job. Most stylist work is freelance and is awarded based on whom you know and how well you get along with the crew during a photo shoot, editorial meeting, or client meeting. Therefore, a strong networking ability is an essential skill.

On the Job

Employers

Almost all employers—fashion magazines, online and print fashion companies, and film and television producers—hire fashion stylists on a freelance or contract basis. With the decline of the fashion magazines, very few full-time positions are available.

Working Conditions

Although most stylists work in an indoor environment during photo shoots, traveling to various locations for meetings, photo shoots, and to look at and obtain clothing is integral to the job. More plum jobs may require international travel. Work hours are typically long and very irregular. Stress can be mild if a stylist works for an online catalog, for example, and extreme if he or she works on a fashion show or shoot with a limited budget and tight timelines.

Earnings

The Fashion School's website lists that a midlevel career position can carry the title of assistant fashion stylist and have a salary range from $500 to $5,000 a day. The BLS discloses a median salary of about $64,500 a year for those with a fashion design background. A talented stylist with formal education who has gained experience and has built a portfolio of jobs can attract more lucrative jobs. The BLS states that the highest-paid professionals with a fashion design background can earn in excess of $130,000 annually, but this would be rare, even for a top-level stylist.

Opportunities for Advancement

Rather than linear, advancements in this career are usually signified by having more regular bookings with more regular clients. Stylists consider the more important jobs as ones where they can work with great photographers, great fashions, or celebrity clients. If a stylist is lucky enough to work with another fashion designer or stylist who is considered well known or important, it can cement a budding stylist's career.

What Is the Future Outlook for Fashion Stylists?

Since stylists largely obtain better work through their own hard work, perseverance, dedication, and networking, the future outlook is more on a career-by-career basis then as a national trend. While the fashion industry is seeing an uptick in personal stylists and online catalog work, it is still very much a career built on whether someone's work is seen and noticed. Celebrity stylist Christina Ehrlich built her career on hard work and the willingness to take any job, no matter how unsavory or how low the pay. In the book *In Fashion*, she says, "I did any job I could. I would work sixteen or seventeen hours and get paid $75. . . . But I learned about the etiquette of being on set, the art of looking at clothes on a hanger versus on a person, how to do returns, how to be organized. If you don't have someone who gives you a break, you have to just plug along."

Find Out More

Association of Sewing and Design Professionals, Inc.
2885 Sanford Ave. SW, #19588
Grandville, MI 49418
phone: (877) 755-0303
website: www.sewingprofessionals.org

The association's mission is to support individuals engaged in sewing and design-related businesses in both commercial and home-based settings. Its members are involved in professional sewing in a variety of garment sewing specialties, including custom clothing, formal and bridal wear, design, pattern making, tailoring and alterations, accessories, costumes, wearable art, image consulting, and production sewing.

Association of Stylists & Image Professionals (ASIP)
6A Addison Ave.
Holland Park, London, W11 4QR, England
website: www.asiplondon.com

The goal of ASIP is to provide direct and easy access to the services of personal stylists and image consultants, provide a range of services to members, to help them develop their businesses, and to create an active online and actual community of like-minded image-related professionals to provide mutual support and development.

Fashion Industry Association
phone: (813) 441-9814
website: www.thefia.org

The Fashion Industry Association is an organization devoted to helping fashion industry professionals to network and work together toward success. Its vision is to see independent fashion designers, retailers, manufacturers, models, stylists, photographers, hair and makeup artists, and media building their local markets and creating a culture of cooperative business.

International Fashion Stylists Association (IFSA)
1357 Broadway, Suite 455
New York, NY 10018
website: www.ifsaonline.com
The IFSA promotes economic growth, employment opportunities, training through established programs, and the creation of certification for fashion stylists worldwide. It is the intent of the IFSA to help create a universal set of standards for the styling community. It also hosts an annual International Conference of Fashion Stylists.

Fashion Photographer

Fashion photographers work mostly on a freelance basis. They are paid to make clothing look good. They can work for a variety of clients. High-fashion photographers are the elite of this profession; they receive the highest pay among fashion photographers, but only a limited number of people reach this level. These photographers work for the high-end fashion magazines and advertising agencies. Many other fashion photographers work for mail-order and online catalogs to support themselves, and the work is steadier and the pay more lucrative. Finally, fashion photographers can find work for a number of smaller publications, including newspapers and magazines that sometimes feature fashion. These photographers are almost always part of a team that includes hair, makeup, and clothing stylists; models; art directors; magazine editors; and others.

Making the garments look great in a photograph requires many skills. Photographers have to have good technical photography skills. They must have detailed knowledge of their cameras, lighting, and how to make subtle nuances of the fabric and

At a Glance:

Fashion Photographer

Minimum Educational Requirements
Bachelor's degree or two-year program in photography

Personal Qualities
Artistic; good with people; passion for fashion

Certification and Licensing
Voluntary

Working Conditions
Varies; indoors or outdoors

Salary Range
$42,000 to $69,000

Number of Jobs
56,140 (for all photographers)

Future Job Outlook
4 percent increase; slower than average through 2022

style of the garment appear in a photo. In addition to technical skills, fashion photographers are artists. While the creative team will tell photographers what mood and type of image they need, and will provide the props necessary for the shoot, photographers will also have their own creative ideas. If the clothing brand they shoot has a particular image, photographers need to be aware of that. They need to know how to use lighting, contrast, and special effects to achieve the look and feel of the brand in their photographs.

Fashion photographers can work in an indoor studio or outdoors on location, depending on the job. For example, a women's clothing catalog featuring sports-oriented clothing often wants images that reflect a particular season. During summer, the company may want women models wearing their swimwear while sitting, standing, or paddling on surf boards and in open water. In winter, the company may want women models outdoors snowboarding, skiing, and snowshoeing. The photographer must accommodate these locations and understand how to get a good shot of the model in action while still making sure the customer will be able to see the details of the clothing. This requires technical skill and also an artistic flair to convey the lifestyle of the customer.

These photographers are always working under deadlines, and they usually take thousands of photos, of which they may only use a few. They work so closely with the creative team that it is important to maintain the relationship, as stylists and editors will prefer one photographer over another based on how easily he or she works with the team.

High-fashion and magazine photographers usually have their own studios. These highly paid professionals know fashion and fashion history extremely well. They are experts in the different clothing designers and the styles for which they are known. They also have a good understanding of the history of their profession and of the work and techniques of other fashion photographers. They are the quintessential networkers, keeping in constant contact with their clients and scouting potential jobs. A fashion photographer cannot become lazy about his or her technical skills and must think of new ways to present material and stay fresh because, as model Heidi Klum famously quipped, "in fashion, one day you're in and the next day you're out." Creative directors are always looking for new ways to present their clothing brand and will abandon a fashion photographer they consider stale. This is where networking, personal charm, and people skills can make the difference in this highly competitive field. On the Portable Studios website, fashion photographer Jo Duck talks about how he motivates a client to look at a shoot more creatively: "Often the client will have an idea which may be quite 'by the book', and it's my job to try to meet with them in pre-production and get them inspired and excited to try something new. I'll do a lot of research into the brand philosophy and try to push their idea into something more exciting or relevant. Sometimes this works and sometimes it doesn't."

Because these photographers are the A team of the fashion world, they have their own creative team that they work with to provide a consistent experience for the clients and themselves. This team not only includes stylists and a creative director but also people who can build and paint the props necessary for a shoot. Their technical skills—including their artistic and visual sense—are highly developed and they are able to make each shoot distinct and fresh. Reputation, often built over years of hard work, is the most important asset of an elite fashion photographer. Fashion photographer Adriana Curcio, quoted in the Digital Photography School website, says that part of this skill has to do with preparation and finding continuous inspiration:

> Don't just prepare, over prepare! I never walk on to a set without having a concrete idea of what I'm looking to achieve. I have books, and books of tear sheets of images of lighting, makeup, hair, styling, posing, editing, etc. It's very easy to become burnt out as a photographer, but if you have these books of inspiring images to glance through, I can pretty much guarantee something will catch your eye, and a concept or story will begin to develop.

These elite stars of the profession attend the same fashion media events that other fashion professionals attend, and they are as good at hobnobbing with the other professionals in their field as they are at taking photographs.

To pay the bills, many fashion photographers work for mail-order and online catalog companies. High-end fashion photographers will also take this work in order to support themselves through dry periods. While such work can be freelance, it is also one of the few areas available for full-time photographers. A catalog job may take days or weeks to shoot. Although the work is full time, usually with benefits and job security, it pays much less, and it has less prestige than high-end fashion photography.

How Do You Become a Fashion Photographer?

Education

Since the profession demands technical knowledge, most budding fashion photographers obtain a bachelor of arts degree in photography or complete a two-year certificate in the subject. Schools offer courses in the technical aspects of photography, including equipment, processes, and techniques. Art schools may offer useful training in photographic design and composition. Fashion photographer Chad Boutin argues on the website All Art Schools that the art school experience offers another important aspect: working with teachers who are also professional photographers. "Find that person who inspires you, and take every class they offer. Instructors are people that mold you and impart information to you. If you find one that inspires and challenges you, stick with that person." However, there are always fashion photographers who master the skills on their own. Dani Diamond, speaking on the SLR Lounge website, talks about how he got into photography: "When I was in business school, a friend of mine walked around with a DSLR [camera]. I asked him to borrow it and after a few days, I bought my own Nikon D90. I've been shooting ever since. I like to think I got the best education the internet can provide but I never went to school to study photography." Because photographers are mostly freelance, many in the field recommend taking courses in business and marketing.

Certification and Licensing

Certificates are offered by the Professional Photographers of America association. A written exam is required to obtain one.

Volunteer Work and Internships

As with other fashion careers, internships are highly recommended. Many art schools offer internships through their career planning and placement office, although internships are also available online. These are highly competitive, and many in the field recommend that budding photographers have a portfolio to present to prospective clients. Almost every fashion professional has interned. In an interview with the website of the British newspaper the *Telegraph*, fashion editor Lisa Armstrong discusses what she looks for in an intern: "Have realistic expectations of what may be asked of you; it's doubtful you'll be asked to style a cover shoot, or be put forward to become America's Next Top Model. It is fair to say that going to the post [mail] room, and packing up luggage for fashion shoots is a reality."

Skills and Personality

A passion for fashion is essential. Photographers who wish to work in high-end fashion must couple highly developed technical skills with a heightened artistic sense. The ability to work well with a team is also important for any fashion photographer. All photographers must be good businesspeople, be great organizers, possess good management skills, and work well with people—both the client and the creative staff. This entails keeping an open mind and allowing other creative people input into shoots. Jo Duck claims that allowing the entire creative team to contribute to the shoot allows him to be successful:

> I'm very big on pre-production and find it's a thrilling component to putting together a good editorial fashion shoot. An idea will come find me, I'll mull it over, get my notebook out, watch films with a similar style or mood, listen to music which emphasizes the idea and then start getting a crew of stylists, make-up artists, models, hair stylists & assistants together who I think will be as enthusiastic about the idea as I am. Then they all change it slightly with their own interpretations and that's where the shoot can reach its potential.

Many in the fashion world also consider hard work and persistence to be key traits of a great fashion photographer. One of the most famous fashion photographers of all time, Mario Testino, interviewed on Style.com, concurs: "It's very difficult to take a good picture. The technique is almost the smallest part of it. The experience of art, how to get what you need out of people, how to work with a stylist—there are a lot of things that you have to do many times. It's really true that practice makes perfect."

Employers

Fashion magazines such as *Elle, Marie Claire,* and *InStyle*; catalog companies; and newspapers all hire fashion photographers. Other employers include photography studios that specialize in fashion.

Working Conditions

Working conditions vary greatly. A photographer can work indoors in a studio or outside on location on photo shoots. All photographers spend time at a computer, retouching and uploading their photographs. Photographers who work full time on catalogs spend a lot of time at their computers.

Earnings

According to the website Indeed, fashion photographers' incomes vary depending on where they live. They earn between $52,000 and $69,000 per year in the northeast region, with lows in Pennsylvania and highs in New York. In the west region, they earn lows of $42,000 in Hawaii and highs of $65,000 in California. Fashion photographers make $49,000 to $69,000 per year, respectively, in Louisiana and Mississippi, which represents the low and high salaries in the south region. And those in the midwestern region earn from $46,000 to $62,000, respectively, in South Dakota and Illinois.

High-end fashion photographers can earn much more, though the competition is fierce and jobs are few. They can make $250,000 to $500,000 in billings, though their net will be much less.

Opportunities for Advancement

Almost all fashion photographers start out as an assistant to a fashion photographer. More than half of all fashion photographers are freelance. Advancement comes from getting more prestigious work and from being hired as a primary photographer on a project. Competition is fierce, so the ability to work with a prestigious photographer or studio is highly valued and difficult to obtain. Catalog photographers also start out in the assistant role, but only the best move up to a staff photographer position.

What Is the Future Outlook for Fashion Photographers?

According to the BLS, employment of freelance and full-time photographers (including fashion photographers) is projected to grow 4 percent through 2022, slower than the average for all occupations. The BLS expects growth to be limited due to the decreasing costs of getting into the profession because of digital cameras and the added competition offered by amateur photographers and hobbyists.

Find Out More

American Photographic Artists (APA)
2055 Bryant St.
San Francisco, CA 94110
phone: (800) 272-6264, ext. 10
website: www.apanational.com

The APA is a national organization for professional photographers; it believes in elevating photographic art and works to protect content. The association provides access to the most progressive local programming, powerful national legislation, prestigious mentorships, affordable insurance options, and collective industry benefits.

Photographic Society of America (PSA)
3000 United Founders Blvd., Suite 103
Oklahoma City, OK 73112
phone: (855) 772-4636
website: www.psa-photo.org

The PSA promotes the art and science of photography as a means of communication, image appreciation, and cultural exchange. The society provides education, information, inspiration, and opportunity to all persons interested in photography. The PSA fosters personal growth and expression, creativity, excellence, and ethical conduct in all aspects of photographic endeavor.

Professional Photographers of America (PPA)
229 Peachtree St. NE, Suite 2200
Atlanta, GA 30303
phone: (404) 522-8600
website: www.ppa.com

The PPA is the world's largest nonprofit photography association organized for professional photographers by professional photographers. The PPA offers educational workshops and classes on a variety of photographic techniques. It also is a resource for those who own photography businesses.

Society for Photographic Education
2530 Superior Ave., #403
Cleveland, OH 44114
phone: (216) 622-2733
website: www.spenational.org

The Society for Photographic Education is a nonprofit membership organization that provides and fosters an understanding of photography as a means of diverse creative expression, cultural insight, and experimental practice. Through its interdisciplinary programs, services, and publications, the society seeks to promote a broader understanding of the medium in all its forms through teaching and learning, scholarship, and criticism.

Interview with a Textile Designer

L ynne Haas is a clothing textile designer for Patagonia, an outdoor clothing and gear company. She works in the company's Southern California office. She was interviewed by telephone.

Q: Why did you become a textile designer?

A: From childhood, I looked around at all of the fabric and thought about how beautiful it was. My family was an artistic family. My grandfather was a screenwriter, and my father designed museum exhibits. I learned to weave on a loom with my grandmother when I was a child. My grandmother was a true artist. We did lots of art together, we painted, made rugs, wall hangings—lots of projects. She lived next door to a master weaver who had a variety of looms, and my grandmother and I would go over there and learn to weave. My first weaving project was a saddle blanket I loomed for my pony.

My love of fabric design lay dormant through my teen years, but when I was deciding on a college I started looking at becoming a textile designer. I looked at schools that offered a program in textile design. I was especially interested in a program that offered the artistic and the technical side—how fabric is woven, working with mills, looms, etc.

Q: Can you describe your typical workday?

A: The work is always geared around a season. At Patagonia we have a fall and a spring season. Unlike other companies, Patagonia is not focused so much on fashion trends. We are trying to make a garment that becomes someone's favorite garment for years. We are always working two years ahead. Since the garments are guaranteed for life, we have to make sure the fabric and sewing are very high quality. The process works something like this: At Patagonia, the merchandiser is the one that decides on the number of new garments that will be made for a particular season. I worked in menswear, so, for example, the merchandiser might say that we need four shirts, three pairs of pants, two belts, and two pairs of shorts for the season. The creative director decides on what color palette the collection will have. The director uses information given to him from the salespeople and the merchandiser, as well as past sales. He might say the color palette is going to be green and blue, and that we need a black or charcoal option, etc. This is communicated to the apparel designer and textile designer at a design brief.

The work is very collaborative. A textile designer is paired with one or two apparel designers. Apparel designers are the ones that decide on the shape of garment. The textile designer is the one that designs the fabric's surface. Next, the designers go on an inspiration trip. They pick a destination like Bali, Chile, India. We spend lots of time outdoors in nature, take photographs. We also do cultural research, looking at the textile history in the country. But we are not looking to re-create the garments of that country, we want to use that history and the place as an inspiration to make a modern-day garment. Patagonia wants garments that are more timeless. For example, one year we took a trip to Munich. We visited a shoe designer that had been in business for fourteen years making these incredible handcrafted shoes. Not because we were designing shoes, but we got the feel of a real craftsperson taking pride in his craft for generations—really inspiring! We also look at other industries that have nothing to do with clothing, such as car design, industrial design, athletic climbing gear, and tools.

After returning from our inspiration trip, I design the textiles from a particular point of view—making sure that all of the textiles go together with each other. There are three different types of textiles I design: yarn weaving, which is woven into fabric; print design, which is silk-screened on the surface of the fabric; and knit, which is what is used in beanie caps. I come up with a croquis—this is the industry term—it means a sketch of the design. A textile designer has to both have great drawing and artistic skill and also math skills. I need to figure out when the pattern will repeat, for example, so that the repeat isn't obvious on the garment itself. I then take that design and use computer software to generate it digitally. Then I add color. Color is also one of the expenses of fabric, so we try to limit the number of colors. The textile designer figures out what's called the colorway—how the colors will be blended together. So, for example, a garment will have the same pattern but in three different colors. Everyone has input on the design, the merchandiser, sales people, it's a definite collaboration, and a democratic process.

The designs then go to the mill, and they make an attempt, called a strike off, to try to match what we have designed. We can then see how the yarn takes the color you designed, for example, or how the fabric actually looks after it's printed. We usually adjust one or two things, then communicate back with the mill. Here's where you need to have great written communication skills. The mills are all over the world, so we primarily use e-mail to communicate. At this point, we are also under a time crunch, and so it's really important to move these initial stages along. At most, designers get two strike offs, and then we need to get the product on the looms. I need to get this done quickly. These time pressures help teach you to be efficient with your design solutions.

Q: What do you like most and least about your job?

A: I love to see my finished garments on a real person. It's so great to see someone wearing the shirt or beanie you made—it's really fun! I also love the collaboration with people, and love doing the research phase. And I really like the technical side of what I do. I love the challenge of making something beautiful under the constraints of what the machines can do, what the fabric can do, etc. The things I like least are the intense deadlines and the overtime! You are struggling to get something done.

Q: What personal qualities and skills do you find most valuable for this type of work?

A: Good drawing ability and painting ability, a good sense of color, and the technical knowledge to know how your design will be executed. These technical aspects include working out the dimensions of the design, knowing how a textile mill will be working with your design. I think I definitely have an advantage because I have woven fabric. I know what it's like. I think a college education in textiles is essential. Part of the curriculum is to learn how to knit on knitting machines, and a visit to a mill. I also think you need to have a passion for fabric.

Q: What advice do you have for students who might be interested in this career?

A: Develop your fine art ability, then find a really good college program that will teach you the industrial processes. Figure out your specialty. For example, do you just want to design prints? Or do you just want to design woven textiles for home furniture? Do you love painting, but weaving not so much? You can pick a specialty that can allow you to focus on just one of those things. I find there is lots of opportunity for a well-trained textile designer. It's a unique trade.

Other Jobs in the Fashion Industry

Accessory designer
Archivist
Costume supervisor
Creative director
Dyer/colorist
Embroidery designer
Event management
Fabric technician
Fashion curator
Fashion forecaster
Fashion public relations
Fashion shoot producer
Fitting model
Foot model
Footwear designer
Hairstylist
Handbag designer
Hand model
Hat designer
Illustrator
Jewelry designer

Magazine editor
Makeup artist
Marketer
Merchandiser
Pattern grader
Patternmaker
Personal shopper
Print designer
Production manager
Quality-control specialist
Retail store manager
Sales assistant
Showroom sales specialist
Tailor
Teacher
Technical designer
Visual merchandiser
Wardrobe master/mistress
Wardrobe assistant
Weaver
Yarn supplier

Editor's Note: The online *Occupational Outlook Handbook* of the US Department of Labor's Bureau of Labor Statistics is an excellent source of information on jobs in hundreds of career fields including many of those listed here. The *Occupational Outlook Handbook* may be accessed online at www.bls.gov/ooh/.

Index

Picture Credits

About the Author

Bonnie Szumski has been an editor and author of nonfiction books for twenty-five years.